A HANDBOOK
ON
GOOD MANNERS
FOR CHILDREN

A HANDBOOK
ON
GOOD MANNERS
FOR CHILDREN

BY

ERASMUS
OF ROTTERDAM

Translated By
Eleanor Merchant

Published by Preface 2008

10 9 8 7 6 5 4 3 2 1

Copyright © Preface Publishing 2008

Copyright (introduction and translation) © Eleanor Merchant 2008

Eleanor Merchant has asserted her right to be identified as the author
of this work under the Copyright, Designs and Patents Act 1988

First published in Great Britain in 2008 by Preface Publishing
1 Queen Anne's Gate
London SW1H 9BT

An imprint of The Random House Group Limited

www.rbooks.co.uk
www.prefacepublishing.co.uk

Addresses for companies within The Random House Group Limited
can be found at www.randomhouse.co.uk

The Random House Group Limited Reg. No. 954009

A CIP catalogue record for this book is available from the British
Library

ISBN 978 1 84809 108 5

The Random House Group Limited supports The Forest Stewardship
Council (FSC), the leading international forest certification
organisation. All our titles that are printed on Greenpeace-approved
FSC-certified paper carry the FSC logo. Our paper procurement policy
can be found at www.rbooks.co.uk/environment

Designed by Two Associates

Printed and bound by GGP Media GmbH, Pößneck

CONTENTS

Introduction	ix
A Handbook on Good Manners	
for Children	1
The Eyes	5
The Nose	9
The Face	13
The Mouth	17
The Hair	21
Posture	23
Private Parts	25
Sitting	27
Bowing	29
Dress	31
Behaviour in Church	35
Table Manners	41
Meeting People	65
Playing	77
The Bedroom	79
Conclusion	81

A NOTE ON THE AUTHOR

Desiderius Erasmus of Rotterdam (1466/1469–1536) was a Dutch humanist, theologian and classical scholar. A widely acclaimed European 'man of letters', he spent time in England, France, Italy, Germany and the Low Countries. He prepared important new Latin and Greek editions of the New Testament, influential for the Reformation, and wrote many other works, including *Praise of Folly*, *Education of a Christian Prince*, *Adages* and *Colloquies*. His publications reveal his constant devotion to the progress of humanist education as well as a masterful command of sixteenth-century media.

A NOTE ON THE TRANSLATOR

Linguist Eleanor Merchant, BA (Oxon), MA (London), teaches Latin for Early Modern Research at the Centre for Editing Lives and Letters, Queen Mary, University of London. She is writing a doctoral thesis on biography and translation in sixteenth-century England. With three impeccably-behaved hooligans of her own, her interest in manners goes beyond the academic.

INTRODUCTION

'Young bodies are like tender plants, which grow and become hardened into whatever shape you've trained them'

Erasmus, 1530

A recent ITV survey suggested that behaviour amongst young people has reached crisis point. Apparently, 90 per cent of Britons think we are a ruder nation than we were a decade ago and that parents are failing to ensure that children learn proper manners. According to the poll, 73 per cent of us think that manners should be taught at school in an attempt to halt this 'breakdown in society'. The complaint that children's behaviour is spiralling out of control at an unprecedented rate gains daily exposure in the tabloid media.

However, perhaps it's the case that every generation voices a concern that the next generation is becoming a bunch of poorly-disciplined and rude degenerates. Nearly five hundred years ago, Desiderius Erasmus, acclaimed writer, theologian and educationalist from Rotterdam, wrote in a letter to a friend that he was surrounded by ill-mannered people. He complained 'there was no one except one old man who greeted me properly, when I passed in the company of some distinguished persons'. In 1530, already a prolific author with his bestselling *Adages* and satirical *Praise of Folly*, Erasmus, the pre-eminent humanist 'man of letters', published this short treatise 'to teach the manners appropriate to young children'.

The book was written, in stylish and precise Latin, for an eleven-year-old boy from the

Netherlands, Henry of Burgundy, son of the Prince of Veere. Henry was the grandson of Anna van Borssele, a noblewoman whose patronage Erasmus had enjoyed earlier in his career. Erasmus also addressed his work to 'all young people', expressing his hope that it 'be no small spur ... if they glimpse that the offspring of the most distinguished men are devoted to learning from their earliest years and are running in the same race as themselves'.

A Handbook on Good Manners for Children was the first book in western literature devoted to the question of how to behave in society. It contains conventions and rules that had previously been scattered across works on other topics produced during the Middle Ages. One such was the *Cato*, a popular textbook of manners in Latin rhyming couplets dating back to the third century, quoted by Chaucer in *The Canterbury Tales*. Erasmus had published a 1514 edition of the *Cato*.

In *Manners*, Erasmus addressed the ways in which appearance, body language, and behaviour could convey a person's character and mind. For a youth to become a good man he also had to be trained in the liberal arts, a central concept for Christian humanists in the sixteenth century. This education involved reading, translating and discussing 'morally suitable' texts based on classical literary sources. Erasmus suggested that the attainment of that virtue of goodness – *nobilitas* – and the social access that it afforded were achievable through one's behaviour. He recognised that having good manners enables you to get on in life.

Besides demonstrating the values of acceptable behaviour in sixteenth-century Europe, Erasmus's text was cleverly composed for its instruction in Latin, the essential language of a humanist education. His Latin is straightforward, and, whilst the syntax of the piece is often repetitious, its animated vocabulary and use of popular proverb and literary reference provide a linguistic treasury for a pupil expected to express himself with versatility and depth. Through his colourful language, Erasmus recreates the settings of sixteenth-century childhood: a candlelit dining hall, the stone floor of a chapel, a draughty bedchamber. He describes the untrained boy as he pokes his tongue into the bottom of an eggshell to lick out the last of his supper, or sneaking a couple of bones under the table to an affectionate dog; or, chilly in his bed, hogging the covers with no thought for the companion he's supposed to share them with. We hear the rising volume of children bickering over a game, as Erasmus patiently reminds them that it ought to be played for its spirit rather than its result.

The child whose uncouth instinct governs his behaviour is compared to an assortment of creatures – tuna fish, hedgehog, bull, elephant, stork and wolf – as well as the odd mythological beast. We smile at the fidgeting, frowning, sniffing, coughing, yawning, scratching bodily habits; those same ones which parents and teachers have been nagging children about for at least five hundred years. Whilst urging a high standard of behaviour, Erasmus's advice is often humorous, genial and sympathetic – consistent in tone with his assertion that the key to good manners lies in an ability to 'readily ignore the faults of others, but avoid falling short yourself'.

His take on national stereotypes seems surprisingly modern: the shoulder-shrugging Italian, the lip-pursing German, and the curtsying Englishman. Advice not to repeat gossip nor relate embarrassing behaviour seen at a boozy meal reveals a long-established code that what goes on tour stays on tour. Quoting an ancient Greek proverb, Erasmus exclaims, 'I hate a drinking companion with a good memory.'

Yet strikingly different attitudes expose social values very different from ours. Erasmus, often ahead of his time in his support of education for girls, here subscribes to the commonplace view that silence flatters a woman. He depicts rural life as uneducated and ill-mannered – the sixteenth-century vernacular expression is 'all of the carte' – as opposed to urbane, literally city-based, and civilised.

The first English translation of *A Handbook on Good Manners for Children* was printed in 1532, and includes some vivid language long fallen out of use, such as the apt verb used to describe the act of removing mucus, 'to snyt thy nose', a phrase that could have currency among football commentators today. Whilst delicate reference is made to 'the members that nature hath given to be covered', it may be surprising that the advice on dealing with flatulence is 'let him close the fert under colour of a cough'; or that a child who fidgets on his seat risks giving the impression of 'a man that letteth a blaste'.

The book was an educational blockbuster! Copies of the little unbound Latin volume flew from print houses around Europe, and were quickly translated into every European language. Though slight in appearance, *A Handbook on Good Manners for Children* made a lasting impression, appearing at a pivotal moment in social history. Feudal structures and ideas of chivalry and courtesy were gradually receding, as the new Renaissance concept of *civilitas* took shape. In fact, the specific meaning of the English word 'civility' is directly related to the Latin title of this work, the *De Civilitate Morum Puerilium Libellus*.

The book's rapid success shows that it captured a theme very ripe for discussion in the 1530s, and countless versions have appeared since then. With or without acknowledgement of their source, and varying enormously in tone, they chart the shifting attitudes of society. Stern books of seventeenth-century Puritan schooling, with their unsmiling and intimidating lists of rules and precepts have their origin in Erasmus's *Manners*, as do later Victorian publications for parents, in which children are cast as reprobates from birth and are appointed each other's whistleblowers. An eighteenth-century injunction to 'reprove thy companions as oft as there shall be occasion, for any evil, wicked, unlawful or indecent action or expression' maps social values that seem far removed from Erasmus's advice two hundred years earlier: 'if a friend does something wrong without realising it, and it seems important, then it's polite to inform him of it gently and in private.'

'Conduct books' of the sixteenth century have been described as early examples of our self-help books, and today's 'manners industry' continues to mine Erasmus's theme. The latest edition of Debrett's *New Guide to Etiquette and Modern Manners* minds its elbows alongside a range of re-issued, nostalgically packaged 1930s, 40s and 50s books that cheerfully declare it's fun to learn manners. Perhaps the extensive publication of books and blogs on behaviour, etiquette and – its online equivalent – netiquette, on parenting, on how to live, and how to eat, bear witness to widely felt confusion around social expectations today.

As new concepts of social interaction make demands on traditional decorum, are behavioural values again being redefined, as they were five hundred years ago? The various media through which we now reveal our real or virtual selves appear limitless, and online social networks such as Facebook and Bebo are perhaps playing host to another pivotal moment. They are populated largely by generations who readily adapt and share new codes of conduct in response to technological innovation. Does the latest advice that 'you don't have to make friends with people you don't know – think before you poke' require some translation?

If, as Erasmus wrote, good manners allow you to 'readily ignore the faults of others, but avoid falling short yourself', then perhaps they find new expression today in the indulgent smile of a teenager, when she receives a text message from her father, unwittingly typed in upper case and so (according to prevailing digital etiquette) expressed as a shout!

Posters on buses and on the London Underground urge young people to consider their fellow passengers and refrain from antisocial behaviour when eating or listening to music; guidance that Erasmus would no doubt have endorsed. And likewise, as the same posters ask commuters to try to remember what it felt like to be fourteen.

Was it not ever thus?

Eleanor Merchant

Good Manners for Children

Erasmus of Rotterdam greets a child of noble birth and singular hope, the son of Adolph, Prince of Veere.

If that greatest of men, St. Paul, didn't hold back from making himself all things to all men, on three occasions, in order to benefit everyone, how much less should I worry about taking on a child's perspective from time to time in my enthusiasm to help young people?

Just as, a while ago, I applied myself to the early youth of your brother Maximilian, when I was shaping the language of young people, so now I apply myself to your early years in order to teach the manners appropriate to young children.

Not that you need these rules in any major way, since you were first raised from the cradle amongst courtiers, and soon after gained a teacher so famed in refining untrained children. So it's not the case that everything I write is relevant to you, given that you are born of princes and destined for pre-eminence, but that all children might learn these precepts thoroughly and willingly, because they're dedicated to a boy of such impressive fortune and great promise. And it'll be no small spur to all young people, if they glimpse that the offspring of the most distinguished men are devoted to learning from their earliest years and are running in the same race as themselves.

The duty of shaping the young is made up of many parts, of which the first and most important is that the seeds of piety are planted within a child's tender heart. Secondly, that a child may both love and gain a thorough knowledge in the liberal arts. Thirdly, that the child is well-prepared for the duties of life. Fourthly, that from the earliest stage, the child becomes accustomed to good manners.

This last role I have now undertaken as my special duty. For a good many other people (besides myself) have written a lot about the other aspects. Although the external appearance of the body proceeds from a well-ordered mind, we may notice that an otherwise upright and educated man, if taught carelessly, is sometimes lacking in social grace. I don't deny that this outward show of manners is one of the most basic elements of philosophy, but it is, according to current opinion, very useful for gaining good will, and ensuring that those fine gifts of the soul are agreeable to the eyes of men.

It's appropriate for a man to be well composed in mind, body, gesture and clothing. Above all, good behaviour is most important in children, particularly those born into privilege.

And those whose minds are refined by the study of liberal arts can be considered noble. Let other people emblazon their shields with lions, eagles, bulls and leopards; the emblems of the intellect, acquired by an education in the liberal arts, bear a truer nobility.

THE EYES

The cultivated mind of a child is most evident from his expression. So that this is clear to all, the eyes should be steady, respectful, and well set.

Not in a frown, which suggests cruelty; nor staring out shamelessly, an indication of cheek; neither darting and rolling around, signs of insanity;

Nor glancing sideways, the expression of those under suspicion or up to no good;

Nor must they be opened wide apart in the manner of stupid folk; the eyes and eyelids shouldn't blink all the time, indicating instability,

Nor gaze out in astonishment, as if stunned, a look once noted of Socrates.

They shouldn't be too piercing either, as that implies fury, nor over-expressive, which can suggest impertinence, but they should present themselves as a reflection of a calm, respectful and amicable mind.

For wise men from earlier times weren't blind in saying that the seat of the soul is in the eyes.

Indeed old pictures show us that it was once a particular mark of modesty to look around with your eyes half-closed, just as, among certain Spanish people, avoiding eye-contact is considered flattering and amiable. Likewise we know from paintings that, in the old days, lips that were closed and drawn-together were taken as evidence of honesty.

But something that is innately graceful is recognized as such by everybody. That said, it's sometimes appropriate to 'play the polypus' and adapt ourselves to specific local customs.

There are certain qualities of the eyes which nature has granted in various ways to different people. These don't fall into any of our categories of manners, except to say that a poorly-controlled expression often spoils the character and appearance not only of the eyes but of the entire body too. On the other hand, when the demeanour is well-controlled, a naturally pleasing appearance can be set off even more favourably, and a feature that's naturally unappealing will be somewhat, if not entirely, effaced.

It's inappropriate to wink at another person. For what is it other than doing yourself out of an eye? We should leave that gesture to tuna fish and one-eyed mythical metal-workers.

You should keep your eyebrows straight, not furrowed, which implies cruelty. Nor should you raise them too much as it looks arrogant and proud, nor droop them down over the eyes, sign of an evil imagination.

A relaxed and smooth forehead indicates a mind with a clean conscience and a gentle nature: don't let it be knit in wrinkles like an old person, nor waggle up and down like a hedgehog, nor frown crookedly like a bull.

THE NOSE

Don't let your nostrils be full of snot like some grubby person; Socrates was criticized for that vice.

Drying or wiping your nose with your cap or your clothing, or on your sleeve or arm, is a habit only for fishmongers. Not that it's much better to wipe your nose with your bare hand if you're only going to wipe that on your clothes. Rather, it's good manners to remove any dirt from your nose with your handkerchief, and, if more distinguished people are present, to do it with your head turned away.

If any mucus falls on the ground once you've cleared your nose with both fingers, make sure you quickly tread it underfoot.

It's also rude to sniff, and taken as a sign of unpleasantness.

It's rather obscene to snort through your nose, and implies anger if it's a habit. Of course those who are short of breath on account of illness must be excused.

You should avoid speaking with a nasal tone, as this is the practice of horn-blowers and elephants.

Wrinkling your nose is only for scornful types and natural fools.

If you sneeze when others are around, it's polite to turn aside. When you've stopped you should bless your mouth with the sign of the cross, after taking off your cap, and thank (or ask for pardon from) those who said or were about to say 'Christ help you.' (Sneezing, like yawning, often stops you from hearing.)

It's polite to say 'Christ help you' to another person when they sneeze. And a child should raise his cap if others there say 'Christ help you' to another man or woman.

Finally, making a raucous noise or shrieking intentionally when you sneeze, or showing off by carrying on sneezing on purpose, is very ill-mannered.

To try not to sneeze when you need to is the deranged sort of action of someone choosing manners over health.

THE FACE

Let natural and innate modesty, rather than any dyed or artificial colouring, give the cheeks their hue. Even that sense of bashfulness should be controlled, so that it doesn't develop into embarrassment, or suggest indifference, or even that fourth degree of insanity, lifelessness, as the proverb has it. For in some children the feeling is so debilitating that it makes them appear altogether demented. The problem can be mitigated if the child becomes used to being in the company of older people and busies himself in acting out plays.

Puffing out the cheeks is a mark of disdain, whilst deflating them indicates despondency; the former is the characteristic of the boastful Thraso and the latter of Judas the betrayer.

Don't press your mouth tight shut, since it suggests that you're afraid of drawing in someone else's breath, nor should you keep yawning, which is the mark of a numbskull, but your lips should meet, touching each other gently. It isn't very polite to smack your lips together, as if making a clucking sound, although this habit can be excusable in adults of high rank who are trying to make their way through a dense crowd. Whilst whatever they do is appropriate for them, we are shaping the behaviour of children.

If you happen to feel the need to yawn, and you can't turn away or leave, either cover your mouth with a handkerchief or with the palm of your hand, and afterwards make the sign of the cross.

To smile approvingly at every single word or deed is the behaviour of fools; to smile at none, shows a slow wit. It's wrong to smile at obscene words or actions. Raucous laughter and uncontrollable giggles that rock the whole body, and for which reason are known as shaking, are not appropriate at any age, but especially in youth. It's improper for anyone when they laugh to make a neighing noise. It's rude when someone opens his mouth in a wide rictus, wrinkling his cheeks and revealing his teeth as if he were a dog; this is known as sardonic {from the death by laughing after eating Sardinian grass}. But the face should express cheerfulness, without the mouth disfiguring it nor suggesting a lax mind.

These kinds of sayings are only for fools; 'I dissolve into laughter,' 'I burst into laughter,'

'I am dying with laughter.' If something happens that's so funny that you can't help but laugh like this, make sure you cover your face with a napkin or a hand.

To laugh on your own or for no obvious reason is an attribute of the stupid or the insane. If however something of this kind arises, it's polite to explain to others the reason for your laughter. But if you don't consider it appropriate to relate this, make something else up, in case someone thinks that they are the object of the joke.

Biting the lower lip with the upper teeth is ill-mannered and menacing, as is biting the upper lip with the lower teeth.

THE MOUTH

It's absurd to lick your lips repeatedly. Pursing one's lips, as if preparing them for a kiss, used to be considered appealing amongst the people of Germany, according to pictures of them. Sticking your tongue out to mock someone is insulting.

Turn your face away when you spit, so that you don't hit anyone with it or with its splash-back. If a bit of phlegm remains on the ground, tread it underfoot, as I've said before, in case it makes anyone feel ill. If that's not possible wipe the phlegm away with a cloth. To re-swallow your spit is rude; also when someone spits every third word out of habit rather than need. Some people develop the off-putting habit of coughing slightly in between speaking, again not from need but from custom. This is the tendency of liars and those who fabricate deceitful words as they speak.

Others, with even worse manners, belch at every third word, a practice which, if ingrained in youth, will remain in later years. The same applies to clearing your throat and spitting, for which fault Terence's Clitipho is told off by his slave.

If you need to cough, make sure you don't do it in anyone's face, and avoid that fault of coughing more loudly than you need to.

Take yourself off when you're about to be sick, although vomiting is nothing to be ashamed of, unless over-eating has made you sick, which is degrading.

Make sure you keep your teeth clean, but whitening them with fine powder is only for girls. Rubbing them with salt or alum can harm the gums. The Spanish do the same using urine. If something gets stuck in the teeth, don't remove it with your knife or your fingernails like a dog or a cat, nor with your napkin, but use a mastic toothpick, or a feather, or use small bones taken from the drumsticks of cocks or hens.

Rinsing the mouth out each morning with clean water is proper and healthy. To do it too often, though, is silly. I shall mention the exercise of the tongue later on.

THE HAIR

It is uncivilised to leave your hair uncombed. It should be neat, but not shining like a girl's. Make sure it's not dirty with nits and lice. Scratching your head in front of others is not appropriate, just as scratching the rest of your body with your nails is grubby, particularly if it's done from habit rather than necessity.

Don't let your hair cover your brow, nor sit on your shoulders. Ruffling your hair by shaking your head to and fro is the behaviour of frolicking horses.

Combing your left hand through your hair from forehead to crown is not very elegant; it'd be more discreet to part it with the hand.

POSTURE

Stooping your neck and hunching your shoulders is a sign of laziness. Thrusting yourself back the other way suggests arrogance. It's proper to hold yourself upright and relaxed. The neck should tilt neither to left or right (an action only for the mime artist), unless the conversation or some such requires it.

Your shoulders should be balanced evenly, not like sail-yards, where one is raised and the other lowered. If bearing of this kind is neglected in youth, it becomes a natural habit, and deforms the proper posture of the body. In this way, those who because of idleness have acquired the habit of hunching their bodies are making hunchbacks for themselves that nature didn't give them. And those who've become used to holding their head to one side, are so ingrained in this habit that their attempts to change it in adulthood are in vain. For young bodies are like tender plants, which grow and become hardened into whatever shape you've trained them with a pole or cord.

Bending both arms behind your back gives the impression of being sluggish and thieving. It's not much better to stand or sit with one hand on your groin, a manner which seems elegant and soldierly to some. However, what's pleasing to fools is not a good indicator of what's consistent with nature and reason. The rest will be discussed when we come to consider conversation and mealtimes.

PRIVATE PARTS

Revealing without need those parts of the body which nature has covered with modesty is to be completely avoided by anyone respectable. But when necessity requires it, then it should be done with proper bashfulness, even if no one else is there to witness it. For there are always angels present, from whom comes that most welcome sense of shame, as a companion and guardian of chastity in children. It's appropriate for these parts of the body to be hidden from sight, and even more so that they don't come into contact with another person.

To refrain from passing urine is bad for your health, but be discreet when you go. There are some who teach that a child should hold in digestive wind by clenching his buttocks.

But it's not good manners to make yourself ill in your eagerness to appear polite. If you can go somewhere else, then do that on your own. But if not, as the oldest of proverbs goes, 'let him disguise the fart with a cough.' Anyway, why don't those people teach in the same way that children should refrain from moving their bowels, since it's far more damaging to refrain from breaking wind than to constrict the bowels?

SITTING

Sitting with your knees spread, or standing with your legs wide apart or crossed is the stance of a show-off, like Thraso. Keep your knees together when you sit, and your feet together, or just slightly apart, when standing. Some people cross one leg over the other knee while they are sitting; others stand with their legs crossed. The first indicates anxiety, the second is downright absurd. It was the custom of kings long ago to sit with their right foot resting on their left thigh, but that habit is no longer acceptable. Among the Italians, some put one foot on top of the other, in a show of respect, almost standing, stork-like, on just the one leg. I don't know that this style is suitable for children.

BOWING

In making a bow, manners suitable for one place may be unsuitable for another. Some bend both knees equally, others keep their body straight, and others again incline a little. There are those who consider that style effeminate, and instead keep their body straight, and bend first the right knee, then the left, a custom which amongst the English is considered praiseworthy in youth. The French make a measured turn of their body as they bend only their right knee. In these matters, where such variety of custom doesn't conflict with what's decent, it will be acceptable either to follow the style of your own country, or to comply with that of another when foreign manners are more appropriate.

Your gait should be neither feeble nor hasty; the former suggests you are over-sensitive, the latter that you've lost your temper, nor should you weave to and fro. For we leave such silly staggering with a slight limp to Swiss soldiers, and to those who consider it great decoration to wear feathers in their caps. And yet we note that this habit also pleases Bishops.

To play with your feet as you sit is for stupid folk, just as fidgeting with your hands is a sign of a weak mind.

DRESS

You've got the gist of the matter concerning the body; now for a few points regarding dress, since clothing is, in a way, the body's body. It's from their style of dress that we may understand the nature of someone's mind. Not that it's possible to determine this with certainty, since neither fortune nor rank comes equally to all, nor is every person equally good-looking or unsightly, nor are the same things pleasing or displeasing to every generation. And just as in many other matters, it should be taken for granted that, as the proverb has it, it's a wise man who instructs us to be subject to the law, to our country, and to our time.

Yet, even accounting for these variables, there are styles which in themselves are respectable or, rather, not, as for example, those bits of dress which have no function. It's ridiculous for a woman to drag behind her an expansive train; for a man it's reprehensible. Whether it's appropriate even for cardinals and bishops I leave to the judgement of others.

Transparent garments have always been considered improper for both men and women, seeing that another function of clothing is that it conceal those parts which it's immodest to bring into sight.

Once it was considered somewhat effeminate to be without a belt, but nowadays it's not held against you, since the inventions of underwear, shirts and hose cover up the private parts even if your tunic flies apart. Otherwise, clothing that's too short to cover the private parts when you bend over is never decent.

Clothing that's been slashed apart suggests madness. Embroidered or multicoloured clothes are for fools and apes. So make sure your style of dress is in keeping with your means and standing, and well-suited to your country and custom. Don't be conspicuous by your shabbiness, nor by any opulence, wantonness or arrogance.

Lack of concern with their appearance suits young men, so long as it doesn't fall into slovenliness. Disgustingly some people stain the hems of their shirts and tunics, spattering them with urine. Others plaster their chests and sleeves with shameful crusts, not of plaster, but of phlegm from their noses and mouths.

There are those who let their clothes slip off them lop-sided, and others who yank them right up to their kidneys at the back, and some who even think this look is a good one! Just as each piece of clothing on the body should be clean and neat, so it ought to fit properly. If your parents have given you particularly tasteful clothing, you mustn't keep twisting around to admire yourself, showing off and preening yourself in front of others, for one is the habit of apes, the other of peacocks. Let others admire you while you yourself seem unaware of your fine dress. The greater someone's fortune, the more agreeable is his modesty. We should allow those who are less well off the comfort they take in their own moderate pride. But a rich man who flaunts the quality of his clothing, reminds others of their own pitiful state, and kindles the flame of envy towards himself.

BEHAVIOUR IN CHURCH

Whenever you go through the doors of a church, remove your cap, genuflect a little, and turn your face towards the sacrament, acknowledging Christ and the saints. The same should be done, either in the city or out in the country, whenever you come across the image of the cross. Don't pass through a church without at least addressing a short prayer to Christ, with the same degree of reverence, that is, with your head bare and kneeling down.

When mass is being celebrated, ensure the whole bearing of your body is in accordance with this devotion. Keep in mind that Christ is present with countless thousands of angels.

If someone were to approach a mortal king surrounded by his group of courtiers, yet fail to remove his cap or make a bow, he would be considered not just uncivilized, but genuinely mad by all around. If such is the case there, how much worse it is to keep your head covered, and to remain standing in the presence of the king of kings, the giver of immortality, whilst heavenly angels surround him in worship. Nor does it matter if you don't see them, for they see you, and it's no less certain that they are present than if you could see them with your actual eyes. For the eyes of faith are able to discern more clearly than those of the flesh.

It's unseemly when certain people amble around in the church, and 'play the peripatetic'. Porticoes and marketplaces are suitable places for strolling, not churches, which are set apart for sermons, holy sacraments and prayers.

Make sure your eyes remain fixed on the preacher, and your ears likewise attend to him, whilst your mind concentrates on him with every reverence, as if you're listening not to a man, but to God speaking to you through the mouth of a man.

When the Gospel is proclaimed, stand up, and listen with devout attention if you are able. When the Creed is sung, at the words 'and was made man', kneel down, as in this way you submit yourself in honour of him, who, although Lord of all the heavens, came down to earth for your salvation; who, although God, deigned to become man, that he should reconcile you with God.

Whilst the mystery of the sacrament is carried out, compose your whole body in an attitude of devotion, with your face turned towards the altar, your mind towards Christ.

Letting one knee touch the ground, whilst keeping the other up to support your left elbow, is the gesture of those unholy soldiers who jeered at the Lord Jesus, saying 'Hail, King of the Jews!' You must kneel on both knees, with the rest of your body bowing slightly in due reverence. For the rest of the time either read something from your little book, either short prayers or some wholesome teaching, or let your mind meditate on some divine matter.

At such time, to witter nonsense in your neighbour's ear is the conduct of those who don't believe that Christ is present, and it's a sign of insanity to allow your eyes to wander all over the place.

Consider yourself to have come to church in vain unless you go out from there a better and purer person.

TABLE MANNERS

Whilst dining, you should be cheerful, but not cheeky. Don't sit down without having washed, and before that, having trimmed your fingernails, in case any dirt is stuck under them and you are called – dirty-knuckled – as they say, a grimy soap-dodger. Remember, before sitting down, to empty your bladder, or, if need be, your bowels in private. If your belt is a bit tight, it's wise to loosen it a little, but to do that at the table would be considered rude.

As you wash your hands, so too, clear troubles from your mind. For it's not good manners to be gloomy at dinner or to make anyone else miserable.

If instructed to say grace, compose your expression and hands reverently, looking either towards the most senior person at dinner, or at the image of Christ if there's one there. Genuflect at the name of Jesus and the Virgin Mother. If someone else is chosen to say grace, listen attentively and make your response in the same reverent manner.

Willingly give up your seat to someone of higher rank, and if you're invited to sit at a place of greater honour, decline it politely. If then someone in authority repeatedly and earnestly asks you to take that place, comply modestly, so that, in your politeness, you don't appear obstinate.

When sitting down, always keep both hands on the table, not clasped together, nor on your plate. It's impolite to keep one or both hands on your lap, as some do.

Leaning on the table with either or both elbows is acceptable for those who are weak from old age or illness. This habit is also practised by certain spoilt courtiers, who think that everything they do is charming, but should be ignored rather than imitated.

Also, make sure you don't bother the person sitting next to you with your feet. To fidget around in your seat, and to settle first on one buttock and then the next, gives the impression that you are repeatedly farting, or are trying to fart. So make sure your body remains upright and evenly balanced.

If a napkin is provided, place it either over your left shoulder or your left arm. When sitting down to eat with your elders, make sure your hair is combed, leaving your cap off, unless the custom of the place suggests otherwise, or someone in authority, whom it would be rude to disobey, requests it.

In some countries it's the custom that children stand, bare-headed, and take their food at the end of their elders' table. A child shouldn't come near the table unless he is asked, nor should he hang around until the end of dinner but, having eaten sufficiently and removed his plate, he should bend his knee and pay his respects to the guests, in particular to the most distinguished of these.

The cup and small eating knife, properly cleaned, should be on the right-hand side and the bread on the left. Clutching the bread in one hand, and breaking bits off with the fingertips, is a habit limited to certain over-indulged courtiers. You ought to use your small knife to cut your bread, not tear the crust apart or cut at it from both sides, which is the habit of those who are spoilt. In the olden days men used to handle their bread reverently at every meal, as if it were a sacred object, which is why we sometimes have the custom of kissing the bread if it has accidentally fallen on the floor.

To begin a meal straight away by drinking is the way of heavy drinkers, who gulp drink down not because they are thirsty but out of habit. This practice is not only morally demeaning, it also interferes with the health of the body.

Nor should you drink straight after having a mouthful of soup, even less so after having milk.

For a child to drink more frequently than two or, at the most, three times during dinner, is neither appropriate nor healthy. You should have a drink at some point after you've begun the second course, especially if it's a dry food. Then again at the end of dinner, sipping it gently, rather than swilling it down slurping like a horse.

Both wine and beer (which is as inebriating as wine) are as harmful to children's health as they are unsuitable. Water suits the energy of youth, but if it's not available, or if the nature of the region or some other reason makes it impossible, then weak beer should be used, or a light wine, diluted with water.

Otherwise the rewards of enjoying strong wine will be decayed teeth, bleary eyes, dim vision and a dull mind, in short, a premature decline.

Before you take a drink, finish chewing your food. Don't put your lips straight to the cup, without first wiping them with a napkin or small cloth, particularly if someone is offering you a drink from their own cup, or when you are sharing a common cup.

It's rude to look around you as you drink, in the manner of a stork turning his neck round towards his back, in case you leave a drip at the bottom, which is impolite.

It's courteous to return the favour when someone toasts you with his cup, raising the cup to your lips, sipping a little and giving the impression of drinking. This will be sufficiently polite to someone who is teasing a little.

If someone crudely urges you to drink more, it's fine for you to promise that you will respond to his request when you are grown up.

Some people, no sooner than they've sat down, immediately stick their hands into the dishes of food. This is the manner of wolves or of those who devour meat straight from the pot before the sacrifices have been made, as the proverb goes.

Don't be the first to touch the food when it's put on the table, not only because it will show you to be greedy, but also because it can sometimes be risky, since someone who puts scalding hot food in their mouth without testing it first, is either forced to spit it out, or if he swallows it, to burn his throat. Either way he is silly and miserable.

A child should be kept waiting for a while, so that he gets used to controlling his appetite. Socrates kept himself in check with this piece of advice, never taking a drink from the first bowl offered, not even as an old man.

If a child is sitting at the table with his elders, he should help himself last, not reach for the pan before it has been offered.

To shove your fingers into dishes with sauce is very rude, but you should pick up what you want with a knife or fork.

Nor should you take bits from all over the dish, as greedy folk tend to do, but you should select the food that's in front of you, as can be learned from Homer, who often uses this line: 'They plunged their hands into the dishes lying ready in front of them'. But if that portion (in front of you) is particularly fine, then leave it for someone else, and take what's nearby.

Just as it's a sign of greed to thrust your hand into every part of the dish, so it's just as rude to turn the dish around so that the best bits come your way. If someone else offers you a particularly choice piece of food, you should try to decline gently before accepting it, but only cut off a small portion for yourself, and offer the remainder to the person who gave it to you, or share it with someone sitting near you.

Food that you can't take with your fingers should be put on your plate.

If someone offers you a piece of cake, or a spoonful of pie, either accept it straight onto your plate or take what is offered on the spoon and when you have put the food onto your plate, return the spoon.

If the food offered is very runny, eat it from the spoon and only return the spoon after wiping it with a napkin.

It's just as rude to lick greasy fingers as it is to wipe them on your clothing. Use a cloth or napkin instead.

To swallow whole pieces of food in one gulp is the practice of storks and clowns.

If something is being cut up by someone else, it's rude to stretch out your hand or plate before the person serving offers it, in case you seem to be snatching a portion intended for someone else.

The food provided should be taken either with three fingers, or by holding out your plate.

If something is offered which doesn't agree with your stomach, be careful that you don't speak like that comic character Clitipho, 'I can't possibly, sir!', but say thank you politely. For this is the most civilised way of declining. If he continues to offer it, say modestly either that it doesn't agree with you, or that you wouldn't like any more to eat.

The correct way to cut up food should be learnt from a young age, not too scrupulously, as some do, but politely and appropriately. For the shoulder joint should be carved in one way, the haunch in another, the neck in another, the ribs in another; a capon in one way, a pheasant in another, a partridge in another, and a duck in another. However, to give the separate methods here for carving each one would be too lengthy and not worth the trouble. This can be given as an overall guide. It's the style of those (excessive gourmands) like Apicius to scrape off whatever appeals to their palate from every side of the joint.

It's pretty poor show to pass off to another something you've already bitten into.

It's rude to dip a piece of bread that you've already gnawed into the soup.

And it's likewise bad manners to take from your mouth a piece of food that you've been chewing and put it back on your plate. If you do happen to have taken something that you're unable to swallow, turn aside and discreetly throw it away.

It's wrong to pick at half-eaten food or bones once they've been on the side of your plate. Don't make the floor dirty by throwing bones or similar leftovers under the table, nor fling them onto the table-cloth, nor put them back in the dish, but put them on the edge of your plate, or in the dish that's sometimes put out for leftovers.

It's considered tactless to offer food to strange dogs at the table, and even ruder to stroke them during dinner.

It's absurd to pick an eggshell clean with your fingernails or thumb, and even sillier to do this by sticking your tongue in it. It's more polite to use a small knife.

Gnawing on bones is for dogs; using a knife to strip meat away is well-mannered.

It's said, by common jest, to be a mark of vulgarity to take a pinch of salt from the salt cellar using just your fingers. You should take only the salt you need on a small knife. If the salt is out of your reach, you should request it holding out your plate.

Licking a plate or dish which is sticky with sugar or something sweet is something cats do, not people.

Make sure you cut your meat into small pieces on your plate before picking up your bread, and chew them both for a while before you let them go down. This is not only conducive to good manners, but also to good health. Some people gulp down rather than eat their food, rather like someone who, as they say, is about to be taken off to prison.

Greedy gobbling is the way of ruffians. Some cram so much into their mouths at once that their cheeks swell out on both sides like a pair of bellows. Others, chewing with their mouths wide open, make piggy noises. Some people, in their eagerness to scoff their food, snort through their noses as if they are being strangled.

To drink, or to speak, when you have a mouthful, is neither proper nor safe. Steady eating should occasionally be interrupted by intervals of conversation.

Some people eat and drink without interruption, not because they're particularly hungry or thirsty, but because they can't control their actions any other way, unless they scratch their head, or pick at their teeth, or wave their hands around, or play with their knife, cough, or clear their throat noisily, or spit. This kind of behaviour, based on a rather coarse sense of shame, gives the impression of some kind of insanity.

When listening to the conversation of other people, if you're not given a chance to speak, you should avoid giving any indication of boredom. It's rude to sit at the table lost in thought. You may see just such people who, struck senseless, neither hear what others say nor notice that they're eating, and if you call them by name, they seem to wake up as if from a sleep. In such a way their entire mind has been lost amongst the dishes.

It's uncivilised to let your eyes roam about looking at what everyone else is eating, and it's indecent to stare directly at anyone else at dinner for too long. It's even worse to glance sideways shiftily at those sitting on the same side as you. It's worst of all to twist your head round behind you to see what's going on at another table.

To blurt out what someone's said or done when they've had a few drinks is behaviour fitting for no one, especially a child.

A child sitting with his elders should never speak unless either necessity demands it or he's invited to do so. He should smile a little at pleasant talk, but not at all if the conversation is obscene. However, he mustn't frown if the person who has spoken in this way is of higher rank, but should control his facial expression, so that he appears either not to have heard, or at least not to have understood. Silence suits a woman, and even more so a child.

Some people reply before the other person has finished speaking, and it often turns out that by replying to a different question they make a fool of themselves, so that the old proverb applies, that is, 'I was looking for sickles but, another who didn't understand, said they did not have any boats', his response making no sense. Look at the proverb. That wisest of kings teaches this, that it's a mark of foolishness to reply before you've heard. For he who doesn't understand doesn't hear. But if you don't grasp what someone's saying, you should remain silent for a little while, until the person who's speaking chooses to repeat himself. If he doesn't do this, but looks for an answer, you should politely beg his pardon, and ask him to repeat it once more. When you have understood the question, you should pause a little, and then reply in a few pleasant words.

At dinner nothing should be blurted out that might darken the cheerful tone. Harming the reputation of someone not present is a great offence. And it's not the place to reopen old wounds with anyone.

To criticise the meal put before you is considered extremely rude; it's most ungrateful to your host.

If the meal is being supplied at your own expense, just as it's proper to excuse the simplicity of the food prepared, so praising it or remarking on how much it cost is really sour sauce to your guests. Finally, if at dinner someone does something rather uncivilised through ignorance it should be overlooked politely rather than laughed at. Get-togethers ought to feel relaxed.

It's disgraceful to bring out into the open, as Horace says, something that someone has revealed unwittingly. Whatever is said at dinner should be as if written in the wine, so that you don't hear 'I hate a drinking companion with a good memory'. Look at the proverb. If the dinner goes on later than is suitable for a child of your age, and seems to be degenerating, as soon as you feel you've had enough, either discreetly or having made your excuses, take yourself off.

Those who force children to fast, in my opinion, are just as insane as those who stuff children too full of food. For, as the former undermines the slight strength of a tender young body, so the latter overwhelms the mind. Moderation ought to be learnt from the beginning. A child should be fed little and often, and kept short of being completely full up. Some children don't know when they're full, unless their stomach is so distended that they're in danger of bursting, or that they lighten their load by being sick.

Those who often allow their children to stay up through long meals lasting into the middle of the night show their disregard for their children. So if you need to get up from a dinner that's gone on for too long, pick up your plate with its leftovers, and acknowledge the man who seems the most distinguished guest at the table, then the others, and head off. But make sure you come back a little later, in case you seem to have got down just to play or for another reason that seems short of polite. On your return, wait in case something is needed, or stand near the table respectfully, watching in case someone asks for something. If you put something down on the table or remove something, take care not to spill soup on anyone's clothing.

When you're going to snuff out a candle, first remove it from the table, then either dip it straightaway into sand, or step on it with your shoe, so that no unpleasant smell offends the nostrils. If you reach for or pour something, make sure you don't use your left hand.

When you're requested to give thanks, compose your expression to show that you are ready, until the guests are quiet and a good moment for speaking arises. In the meantime keep your face turned respectfully and steadily towards the head of the table.

MEETING PEOPLE

If someone who deserves your respect on account of his seniority, or reverence due to his calling, or who is dignified by his rank, should come along the road, then a child should remember to give way, and remove his cap respectfully, and even make a slight bow or curtsy. You mustn't think, 'Why should I have anything to do with this stranger, who's never done me any good?' You're not paying respect just to the man, to the worthy, but to God.

Just as God bid us, through Solomon, that we should stand up out of respect for the elderly, and likewise, through Paul, he urged us to show double reverence to our elders.

In short, to pay respect to all who deserve it, even the heathen magistrate. And if the Turk himself should rule over us (perish the thought), we would be committing a sin if we denied him the respect owed to that magistrate.

I say nothing at this point about one's parents to whom, second only to God, we owe the highest respect. Nor do we owe any less to teachers, who, since they shape the minds of men, in a way also raise them. And amongst one's peers that saying of Paul ought to have its place, 'defer to each other with mutual respect'.

He who defers to his equal or inferior is not, by doing that, demeaning himself, but is more civil and therefore more worthy of respect.

We should speak respectfully and succinctly to our superiors; lovingly and kindly to our contemporaries.

When speaking, hold your cap in your left hand, with your right hand placed lightly beside the stomach, or, as is considered even more polite, hold the cap with both hands joined together, thumbs out, covering the private parts. Holding a book or a hat under your arm is considered rude.

A shy manner is acceptable, but only if it suits someone, not if it renders them thunderstruck. You should look at the person you're speaking to with a calm, open expression, not with an overbearing or insolent attitude.

Looking down at the ground, as the beast known as the basilisk does, implies you have a bad conscience. Glancing sideways appears shifty.

Turning your face this way and that is an indication of instability.

It's impolite to keep altering your facial expressions, so that one minute you're scrunching up your nose, the next you're frowning, next you're raising your eyebrows, then twisting your lips, then gaping open your mouth, and shutting it again. These are all signs of a fickle character like Proteus.

It's also rude to shake your head and toss your hair, to cough unnecessarily, to clear your throat noisily, likewise to scratch your head, to pick your ears, to wipe your nose, to stroke your face as if wiping away your shame, to rub the back of your head, and to shrug your shoulders, a characteristic we see in some Italians.

To say no by shaking your head, or to summon someone by jerking your head back, in short, to speak in gestures and nods, whilst sometimes fitting for a man, is less appropriate for a child.

It doesn't suit someone of good standing to wave his arms around, gesticulate with his fingers, and sway to and fro on his feet, in short to communicate, not with his tongue, but with his whole body, in the manner of turtle-doves or wagtails and magpies.

Allow your voice to be soft and gentle, not clamorous like a farmer's, nor so subdued that it can't be heard by the person you're addressing.

Make sure your speech isn't too rapid, getting ahead of your thought, but calm and distinct. This style of speech can reduce, if not entirely, at least to a great extent, a natural stutter, or stammer, whereas very hasty speech can often bring about such problems which wouldn't have arisen naturally.

Also when speaking it's polite to repeat, from time to time, the correct title of the person you are addressing. Nothing is more honourable or delightful than the name of father and mother; nothing more endearing than that of brother or sister. If a specific title escapes you, then all educated men should be addressed 'respected teachers', all priests, and monks, 'reverend fathers', all contemporaries, 'brothers and friends'.

For the sake of brevity, address all unknown men 'sir' and every unknown woman 'madam'.

It's disgraceful for a child to swear, either jokingly or in earnest. For what is more shameful than that custom in some countries, where even the girls make every third word an oath; 'by the bread', 'by the wine', 'by the candle', 'by whatever'? So the well-raised child should neither use foul language nor listen to it.

Finally, if something shouldn't, in decency, come into view, it's similarly shameful that it be talked about. If it so happens that some private part needs to be mentioned, it should be referred to in a modest circumlocution. Again, if it's the case that a situation described might make someone feel ill, say if someone talks about vomit, or the toilet, or a bad smell, it should be prefaced with 'I beg your pardon'.

If something is to be contradicted, be careful not to say, 'You're not telling the truth', particularly if you are speaking to your elder, but say with respect, 'It was told to me very differently by so and so.'

A well-mannered child won't get into an argument with anyone, not even his contemporaries, but, if a quarrel does arise, he should concede victory or appeal to another to help settle it.

He shouldn't put himself above others, nor boast about what he's done, nor criticise someone else's behaviour, nor disparage the customs and habits of another country, nor reveal a secret he's been trusted with, nor spread fresh rumours, nor damage someone's reputation spitefully, nor reproach someone on account of an inborn defect. For that kind of behaviour is not only insulting and cruel, it's also stupid. It's as if someone called a man with only one eye 'one-eyed man', or someone with bandy legs, 'bandy-legged man', or someone with a squint, 'cross-eyed man', or an illegitimate person 'bastard'. Following these guidelines should mean that you win praise without envy and gain friends.

It's impolite to interrupt a speaker before he's finished telling a story.

Don't get involved in quarrels with anyone, and show affability to all.

However, choose and take on a few, more intimate friends. But you shouldn't entrust to anyone something you wish to keep quiet. For it's absurd to expect someone else to stay silent about a secret that you're unable to keep to yourself. There's no one who is so self-contained that he has nobody to share his secret with.

It's safest to confide nothing that would embarrass you if it were spread around.

Don't be too inquisitive about other people's business, and if perhaps you catch sight of or overhear something, act as if you know nothing. It's rude to pry or read letters that haven't been shown to you.

If by chance someone opens his letters in your presence, take yourself off. For it's tactless to look on, and even ruder to scrutinise them. Likewise, if you get the impression that a conversation between others is becoming more private, move away discreetly, and don't intrude upon such a conversation uninvited.

PLAYING

When playing games be cheerful. Don't be stubborn, as that causes quarrels.

Likewise avoid cheating and fibbing, since it's from these basic habits that more serious flaws develop.

Someone who concedes a game with good humour gains more honour than one who always insists on winning.

Don't contradict the umpires.

If, when you play against someone less experienced, you always win, let yourself sometimes be beaten, to make the game more fun.

If you are playing with those less privileged than you, don't show your awareness of your superior position.

The point of playing is in the spirit of the game rather than any prize.

They say that children's temperaments are most apparent when they play. If someone is prone to cheating, lying, quarrelling, angry outbursts, or arrogance, it's when he plays that these faults come to light. It follows that a boy of good character should be true to himself just as much in playing as when he's feasting.

THE BEDROOM

In the bedroom, silence and modesty are to be encouraged. At least, shouting and noisy chatting are inappropriate, and even more so when you're in bed.

When you undress or get up, remember to be modest: take care not to reveal to others what custom and nature prefer to be covered up.

If you share a bed with a companion, lie there quietly, don't fidget and throw off your bedclothes, nor annoy him by grabbing his covers.

Before you put your head on your pillow, make the sign of the cross above your head and chest, and commit yourself to Christ with a brief prayer.

Do the same thing in the morning when you first get up, making a good start to the day with a short prayer. For there's no better way to begin the day.

When you've been to the toilet, don't do anything else until after you've washed your face and hands, and rinsed out your mouth.

CONCLUSION

For those lucky enough to be born into privilege, it's disgraceful if their manners don't match their position. Those whom fate has chosen to be ordinary, common, or uncouth have to make a much greater effort with their manners to compensate for their lack of privilege.

No one can choose their own parents, or where they come from, but everyone can shape their own character and behaviour.

I shall end with a short maxim, which seems to me to be of the utmost importance:

The key to good manners is that you should readily ignore the faults of others, but avoid falling short yourself. For that reason, you shouldn't look down on a friend if he has poorer behaviour. Some people compensate for their lack of manners with other qualities. Not that I mean to suggest that no one can be a good person without proper manners; but if a friend does something wrong without realising it, and it seems important, then it's polite to inform him of it gently and in private.

In whatever way this may be of service to the fellowship of all children, my dearest boy, I wish it to be imparted through you, so that, by this gift, you may straight away win over the hearts of your fellow troops and at the same time present the pursuits of the liberal arts and good manners as agreeable. May the grace of Jesus make you worthy to serve, and constantly carry you on to even greater honour.

Freiburg im Breisgau, March 1530

DE CIVILITATE MORUM PUERILIUM LIBELLUS

Pages from the 1534 edition of Erasmus's *De Civilitate Morum Puerilium Libellus*, showing the parallel Latin and English texts. The translator was Robert Whittington, Poet Laureate, and this edition was printed by Wynkyn de Worde at his press in Fleet Street, London.

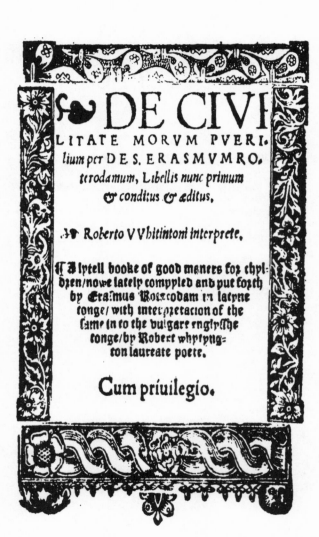

DE CIVI

LITATE MORVM PVERI.
lium per DE S. ERASMVM RO.
terodamum, Libellis nunc primum
& conditus & æditus,

Roberto VVhitintoni interprete.

¶ A lytell booke of good maners for chyl-
dren/nowe lately compyled and put forth
by Erasmus Roterodam in laetyne
tonge/ with interpretacion of the
same in to the vulgare englysshe
tonge/by Robert whytyng-
ton laureate poete.

Cum priuilegio.

ERASMVS

Roterodamus generoso cum
primis & optimi spei puero
Adolph, principis Ve-
riani filio S.

I ter maximū illum
Paulum non piguit
oīa fieri omnibus,
quo pdesse posset omnibus,
quãto minus ego grauari de-
beo tuuãde iuuētutis amore
subinde repueruascere. Itaq́
quē admodū pride ad Maxi-
miliani fratris tui primam
adolescentiam memet accom
modaui, dum adulescentulo-
rum formo linguam: ita nũc
me ad tuam attempero pue-
ritiam, de puerorum moribus
precepturus: nõ qd tu hisce
prescriptis magnopere ege-
as, primum ab incunabilis
inter aulicos educatus, mox
nactus tam insignem for-
mãde rudis ætatis artificem:

Erasmus Roterodam
saluteth a chylde of no-
ble bloode and of sin-
guler hope/named
Adolph, sonne
vnto the
prince of Me-
rian.

F that Paule
very excellente
was not abas-
shed to be made
after al fasshons
to euery person/
to the ende he myght pro-
fyte all fasshons al menne/
howe moche lesse ought I to
be greued to play the chylde
agayne in lyke case/for loue
to helpe youthe. Therfore
lyke as late I applyed my
selfe to the youthe of Mari-
milpan thy brother (whyles
I fasshyoned the tongue of
yonge chyldren) so nowe I
applye my selfe to thy chyldhode / and shall teache the
maners of chyldren: Nat by
cause thou nedest these pre-
scriptes and rules/ brought
vp at the begynnynge of an
enfant amonge courtyers/
after that obtaynyng so notable a mayster to fasshyon
youthe rude and ignorante/

āut qd omnia quæ præscribe
mus, ad te pertineant, & è
principibus, & pricipatui na
tum sed ut libēllus hæc edis
cant omnes pueri, ꝙ am-
plissimæ fortunæ, summæꝗ
spei puero dicata sint. Nec
enim mediocre calcar addet
uniuersæ pubi, si cōspexerit
beroũ liberos à primis statim
annis dicari studijs, & in eo-
dem cũ ipso stadio currere.

Munus aũt formādi pueri
tłi multis constat partibus,
quarũ sicuti prima ita preci
pua est, ut tenellus animus
imbibat pietatis seminaria:
proxima, ut liberales disci
plinas & amet, & perdis-
cat: tertia est, ut ad uitæ of-
ficia instruatur: quarta est,
ut à primis statim æui rudi
mēcijs ciuj ítati morũ assues-
cat. Hanc postremā nunc mi-
hi proprie sumpsi. Nā de su-
perioribus quũ alij cōplures

oz foz bycause ai that I shal
wzite pertcyneth to the/ and
that arte come of pzinces/
and bozne to pzincipalyte/
but foz that ende that all
chyldzen shall moze coura-
gyously lerne this thynges/
bicause it is dedycate to the
a chylde of great possessyon/
and of synguler hope. Moz
it shall nat gyue to all youth
a dull spurre / if they se noble mens sonnes to be fully
gyuen to lernyng fro chyld-
hode/ and renne in the same
rase with them.

The offyce of fassyonynge
of chyldhode resteth in many partes/ of the which that
whiche lyke as it is fyrste/
so it is chefe: That is/ the
tendze wytte shall dzinke
the sedes of loue to god
and his parentes. Secunde-
ly that he shall loue and
lerne the lyberall scyence.
Thyzde/ that he shall be in-
structe to the ozder of his
lyuyng. Fourth that fro the
fyrst rudyment of youthe he
shall be eccustomed to cyuy-
lite and nozture. This laste
nowe I haue take vpon me
as a thing propre/ foz the
other thze bothe many other

A 2

tu nos quoq̃ p̄ multa scripsi-
mus. Quanq̃ aũt externũ il-
lud corporis decorũ ab ani-
mo bene cõposito pficiscitur
tamẽ incuria præceptorũ nõ
nunq̃ fieri uidemus, ut hãc in
terim gratiã in probis & e-
ruditis hominibus desydere-
mus. Nec inficior, hanc esse
clarissimã Philosophiæ par-
tẽ, sed ea, ut sunt hodie mor-
taliũ iudicia, plurimũ cõdu-
cit & ad cõciliandã beneuo-
lẽtiã, & ad præclaras illas a-
nimi dotes oculis hominũ cõ-
mẽdãdas. Decet aũt ut homo
sit cõpositus aĩo, corpore, ge-
stibus ac uestitu: sed ĩ primis
pueros decet oĩs modestia,
& in his præcipue nobiles.
Pro nobilibus aũt habẽdi sũt
oẽs, qui studijs liberalibus
excoliũt animum. Pingãt aľi
in clypeis suis leones, aqui-
las, tauros, & leopardos,
plus habẽt uere nobi'itatis,

and also I haue written many thynges. And al be it this
outwarde honesty of the body cometh of the soule well
cõposed or ordȝed/ natwith-
standyng we se it chaunceth
ofte tymes by neglygence of
maysters that we despȳe (as
a thynge that lacketh) this
grace of honest behauour in
men of nobylite & lernynge.
Nor I denye nat this to be
a very notable parte of phi-
losophy/ but yet that parte
(after the iudgemẽt of men
in this dayes) auayleth gret
ly to alure beneuolens/ also
to represent to the eyen of
men these laudable gyftes
of the soule.
It is semely and fyttynge
that a man be well faspo-
ned in soule/ in body/ in ge-
sture/ and in apparell:and in
especyall it besemeth chyldren all maner of tempe-
raunce / and in especyall in
this behalfe noble mennes
sonnes. All are to be taken
for noble/ whiche exercyse
their mynde in the lyberall
science. Lette other men
paynte in their shyldes Ly-
ons/ Eegles/ Bulles/ and
Leopardes: yet they haue
moȝe of very nobylyte /

q p ī Agnibus suis tot pos-
sunt imagine depingere, quot
plidicerunt artes liberales.
Vt ergo bene cōpositus pueri
aīus undiqz reluceat, relucet
aūt potissimū in uultu sint o-
culi placidi, uerecūdi, cōpo-
siti nō toruī, qd est truculen-
tiæ nō improbi, qd est impu-
dētiæ: non uagi ac uolubiles,
qd est insanæ: nō limi, qd est
suspicioriū et insidias molic-
tium, nec immodice diducti,
quod est stolidoriū, nec subinde cōuetentibus genis ac pal-
pebris, quod est incōstantiū,
nec stupētes qd est attonito-
.riū. id in Socrate notatū. nec
nimiū acres, quod est iracun-
diæ signū. nō innuētes, ac lo-
quaces, quod est impudicitiæ
signum, sed aīm sedatū ac re-
uerenter amicum præ se fe-
rentes. Nec enim temere di-
ctū est à priscis sapientibus,
animi sedem esse in oculis.

whiche for their badge may
paynte so many ymages / as
they haue lerned sure the lyberall scyēce. Than that the
mynde of a chylde well bur-
nysshed may vpon all sydes
euydent apere / for it ape-
reth moste clere in the vy-
sage or countenaunce.

⁋ Of the eyen.

Let the eyen be stable / honest / well set / nat frownyng /
which is syne of crueltie / nat
wāton / which is token af ma-
lapertnesse / nat wandring &
rollynge / whiche is syne of
madnesse / nat twyzinge and
spyeng / whiche is token of
suspection and compasynge
disceyte / nor hāgyng downe
whiche is syne of folly: nor
afterwarde twynklyng with
the browes / whiche is sygne
of vnstablenesse / nor masing
as a mā astonyed (And that
was noted in Socrates) nor
to sharpe / a syne of malyce /
nat makyng synes and pro-
fers nor besy wanton / a token of puell chastyte: but re-
presentyng a mynde well en-
stabled / & amyable with honesty. For it is nat said with
out cause of antyke sage
mē / that the eye is the seate
and place of the soule.